Unraveling Adolescence...

A Journey Through the Maze

Unraveling Adolescence...
A Journey Through the Maze

Anutsek Pathak

Highbrow Scribes Publications
New Delhi

"What an astonishing thing a book is.

It's a flat object made from a tree with flexible parts on which are imprinted lots of funny dark squiggles.

But one glance at it and you're inside the mind of another person, maybe somebody dead for thousands of years.

Across the millennia, an author is speaking clearly and silently inside your head, directly to you.

Writing is perhaps the greatest of human inventions, binding together people who never knew each other, citizens of distant epochs.

Books break the shackles of time.

A book is a proof that humans are capable of working magic."

Carl Sagan, *Cosmos*

Dedicated to

This book is dedicated to all those who are or have been through adolescence, the species that possesses the magical skills to generate emotions at the drop of a hat - frustration, revolt, and the ancient art of eye-rolling. Those who have sailed perilous seas on a regular basis, with the stormy sea of peer pressure and social media on one side and well-intentioned, but bewilderingly archaic Parents on the other.

Contents

From Director's Pen

Congratulations to Anutsek on producing this articulate, reflective and thought-provoking account of the journey so far. Very well-travelled for someone so young and with the experiences of living away from home in a boarding school, Anutsek is well qualified to give his views on the exciting challenges of modern day adolescence.

SDW
Simon David Weale
Director
Bishop Cotton School Shimla

A Message from the Headmaster

I became acquainted with Anutsek in 2021, when he was in class 9, or as it is called at Bishop Cotton School, 'Shell'. As a 'Shellite', Anutsek had already gained the respect of his peers and the attention of his seniors.

A quiet boy, given to introspection without being shy, good at his academics, without neglecting sports, and most importantly for School, always courteous and well mannered, Anutsek was well liked by all who knew him.

I was not particularly surprised to hear that he was writing, though I was a little surprised at his subject matter, a little more mature than I would have expected. The excerpts that I have read only confirm what I already know of his character, and I hope that you, as readers, appreciate his maturity while going through this book and also gain some insight into the facets of life discussed by him.

I wish Anutsek all the best, not only in his maiden attempt at writing, but in whatever he ever chooses to do with his life.

Mathew John
Headmaster
Bishop Cotton School, Shimla

Foreword

Greetings, fellow readers of the written word! Within the following pages of "Unravelling Adolescence," you are about to embark on a young boy's journey, guided by the imagination and creativity of a young author whose spirit knows no bounds. As I read the interesting tales penned by this talented teenager, I am reminded of the raw and unbridled magic that comes with youth. In the following chapters, you will find echoes of his joys, fears, and the struggles that have shaped his journey. Writing this book has been a transformative process and has taught him to confront his insecurities, embrace vulnerability, be himself and find courage in expression. Every word, every phrase, carries a fragment of his essence, laid bare for us to explore. As you continue to flip pages, you will discover a world through the eyes of a young storyteller – a world where possibilities are endless, dreams take flight, and the boundaries of reality are playfully nudged. The author's youthful energy infuses each sentence with a zest for life and a sense of wonder that is truly infectious. As we delve into these narratives, we witness the resilience and determination that only a teenager can possess. The courage to pour one's heart onto paper, unafraid of judgment, is a testament to the power of self-expression and the bravery of embracing one's passions. But beyond the captivating stories lies a profound lesson - that age knows no bounds when it comes to creativity.

The mind of a teenager, untethered by the conventions of adulthood, brings forth a refreshing perspective that challenges us to question, to imagine, and to believe in the extraordinary. Through his episodes and experiences, the author invites us to revisit the essence of youth - the innocence, the naughtiness, the real, the imaginary, the unyielding hope, and the enchantment with the unknown. As readers, we are gifted with the opportunity to rediscover the unspoken dreams we once held dear and to reignite the spark of possibility within our hearts. It is no small feat for a teenager to pen a book, and yet, here we are, witnessing a blossoming talent that has already begun to leave its mark on the literary landscape. With each word carefully crafted (with no intention to hurt), the author invites us to join him on a voyage where the joy of creation knows no bounds.

Dear reader, prepare to be moved and inspired by the tales that await you. Allow yourself to be whisked away by the author's boundless spirit (lively and dampened at times), and as you reach the end of this book, may you be reminded of the incredible potential that lies within every young soul. With admiration for the young mind's inexhaustible creativity with a dash of humour and the bravery to share it with the world, my much-loved student.

May you grow from strength to strength and find joy in all that you do. Looking forward to many more books to read!!

Mrs Rose Lal,
Teacher
Bishop Cotton School, Shimla

Prolouge

It took me a lot of thinking when I was asked to write a foreword for Pathak's essays. Essays that I've been reading and correcting for the past 3-4 years. I've really enjoyed reading them and now when the essays will be complied in a book, I can't wait to read them again.

It is with great pleasure and enthusiasm that I have been invited to write the foreword for this remarkable collection of essays titled "Unraveling Adolescence: A Journey Through the Maze." As I reflect on the turbulent yet transformative period of adolescence, I am reminded of the profound impact it has on shaping our lives and identities. The essays within this book provide a unique and compelling exploration of this critical juncture, offering valuable insights, personal experiences, and expert perspectives that will undoubtedly resonate with readers of all ages. Each one of us has gone through this phase of life .... Or has children or grandchildren who are of this age.

Adolescence is a time of transition, a bridge between childhood and adulthood, where we navigate the labyrinthine complexities of self-discovery, identity formation, and social integration. It is a period characterized by rapid physical, emotional, and cognitive changes, often accompanied by a rollercoaster of emotions and a profound search for meaning.

Unraveling the mysteries of adolescence is no easy task, but the collective wisdom of an adolescent contained in these essays offers a guiding light through the maze.

Furthermore, "Unraveling Adolescence: A Journey Through the Maze" goes beyond merely unravelling the complexities of adolescence; it also offers practical guidance and tools for navigating this transformative phase. The essays are enriched with practical strategies, evidence-based suggestions, and thought-provoking questions that encourage introspection and self-discovery. Whether you are an adolescent yourself, a parent, an educator, or anyone interested in understanding the adolescent experience, this book serves as a valuable resource to help navigate the maze of adolescence with greater resilience and insight and at the same time it's funny too.

As I read through the essays within this collection, I was struck by the power of storytelling and the potential it holds to foster empathy, understanding, and growth. Each essay is a testament to the resilience, creativity, and strength of the human spirit. It serves as a reminder that despite the challenges faced during adolescence, there is tremendous potential for personal growth, self-discovery, and the cultivation of meaningful connections.

All the best to Anutsek for this book and I hope to read many more of his works.

Mrs Alvia Zaidi
Teacher
Bishop Cotton School
Shimla

Review

What is Adolescence? The definition is a period of transition from childhood to adulthood. It includes many physical, cognitive, and psychosocial changes. However, there is very little to nil conversation around what goes into the mind of an adolescent who goes through this transition. In this book, Anutsek talks about this phase and his experiences. When he reached out to me for writing this foreword, I wasn't surprised as I remembered that he indeed, was someone who had a niche for creativity. He has beautifully divided this book into many short chapters, and each chapter felt like a milestone in itself it successfully tries to touch the common syndromes (as the author has called them) which is faced by millions of Gen-Z teenagers. This book tries to educate teens and parents alike about the prejudices, pros and cons of a teen's life.

May life's all best be yours and more power to your pen.

Best Wishes
Mrs Deborah Anthony
Teacher
Bishop Cotton School
Shimla

Preface

There is a young man who lives in the midst of a tumultuous world, where hopes and uncertainties collide. This young man is navigating the maze-like hallways of adolescence, seeking to unravel the mystery of his purpose and identity. This young man is searching for his place in this huge cosmos.

"Unravelling Adolescence - A Journey through the Maze" is the title of this book, and it delves into thoughts and sentiments that have never been stated before. It is frequently stated that one should not allow their thoughts to die because they lack the ability to convey them. Without hesitation, one should always communicate their thoughts using acceptable language and portray feelings clearly and honestly.

No, I'm not hesitant; I'm just not comfortable spending and investing my emotions, opinions, and thoughts with a larger group of people. I've counted some of my closest friends. To solve a problem, I daydream and use my imagination. To rest, I withdraw into my own mind.

I would rather write than speak. Not that I am devoid of the art of oration. I take part in Model United Nations and debates. Engaging in activities such as Model United Nations and debates, they thrive on the intellectual stimulation and adrenaline rush that comes with presenting and defending their ideas. This book beautifully captures my passion for articulating arguments and embracing the challenge of a well-crafted rebuttal.

I am an adventurous introvert with a voracious appetite for books, adventure, and, of course, food (home cooked). I also like calling myself peripatetic. During COVID, I began my reading and writing journey. Without a doubt, my mother is the driving force and inspiration behind this journey.

This journey is intended not only to share my thoughts, acts as a reminder that one does not have to comply to conventional self-expression norms. This book encourages readers to accept their own distinctive communication styles, find consolation in introspection, and embark on their own personal journey of self-discovery.

Eventually, the book conveys the empowering idea that by embracing our passions and truly expressing ourselves, we can inspire others to do the same and find their own confidence, allowing them to navigate the maze of life with courage and self-assurance.

Find YOUR self-assurance and run with it!

Acknowlegment

This book would not have happened had it not been for my mother forcing me to write essays and letters. While my father has been ruthlessly forcing me to mug up the periodic table and the theorems, laws, and the endless formulas, my mother has been urging and ultimately forcing me to write letters to my family members on several occasions. I now realize she has been shaping me for this day.

I have studied in eleven different schools. I have vague memories of Bloom Public School, Vasant Kunj and SpringDales, Pusa Road, the best schools in Delhi. Bishop Cotton School, Shimla is where I have learned and grown. *Grown finely in many aspects.*

In the corridors of learning, a figure stood tall, my erstwhile headmaster Mr. Robinson, inspiring one and all. With wisdom and vision, he graced the school's domain, and brought changes that young minds would forever retain.

He, on every orientation, said to the parents, "You give me a boy, I give you a man." I know not if it is the time, and I have turned into a man, but definitely, I have turned, shaped, and refined to face the world. Mr. Robinson was a tough master and with his stern demeanour and unwavering standards, he commanded respect and instilled discipline among students and staff alike. However, beneath his tough exterior, there resided a profound sense of care and compassion that set him apart as a truly exceptional leader and human being.

Mrs. Asha Sharma was my class teacher in grade 5 at Bishop Cotton School. She has till date been treating me the same way as I was in grade 5, the little lad. She starts with hope you are eating well and ends with come to me should you need anything.

Mrs. Alvia Zaidi, my English and Geography teacher, is not only a fantastic teacher but also a wonderful human being; I look forward to her classes. Mrs Zaidi was my class teacher during the pandemic; she never missed a class and was never even a few seconds late. This attribute of hers has inspired many late risers to get out and about.

She possesses a prodigy in the classroom that is quite unique. A very kind and generous woman, but you better watch your behaviour around her because she won't give you any slack if you act inappropriately. She will graciously shower you with words of wisdom in order to make you understand how and where you have made mistakes. The way she switches between being hot and cold is something that throws off the boys.

Mrs. Deborah Anthony has taught me biology and chemistry for three consecutive years. She has not only taught me the subjects but also lessons I will never forget. I always miss her not teaching in the senior class. She casts a magic spell in her class, wondering how even the ones not very keen about the subject tend not to misbehave. Mr. Anthony now teaches me biology and boys are amazed by his command on the subject. I simply admire how smart a teacher he is, but I hate to say I still miss Mrs. Anthony's classes.

Mrs. Rose Lal is known throughout Bishop Cotton School as the living embodiment of William Shakespeare. She is deft at handling any situation. She coerced me to learn more refined English, which inspired me to improve my skills on a daily basis. Not only does she teach you the tasks at hand, but she also teaches you the tactics of the trade to improve your performance in life. I owe her a great deal.

I owe every bit of my six years spent at BCS to these ladies who hold a very special place and this book has happened because of them. These are the ladies I have been sharing my write-ups with and have always received tons of encouragement in return, for which I will be indebted forever.

I have some buddies who have been with me through thick and thin but know nothing about the book. While I had been writing at odd hours in the dorm or been away from dorm to the chapel, they often asked me what I am up to, I simply used to tell, my mother asked me to write an essay, which was partially true.

I have been taught not to count my chickens until they hatch, so sorry buddies for keeping this a secret. Abhyuday, Aditya, Dhruv, - I have quoted many incidents in this book from our collective incidents. I am confident whenever you read this, you all will comprehend it better than any of my readers.

All three of these men, my housemaster Mr. Rohit Vyas, the warden Mr. Satnam, and my sports teacher

Mr. Gurpreet Sir, have something in common. They never forget to tell me that I am a fauji kid and that I am not allowed to make mistakes; that I must NEVER be late; that I am not permitted to be naughty; and that I am not allowed to come in last place in a race, no matter what.

At times like those, I despise being identified by the name of my father.

My trusted advisor is the Reverend. We share numerous likings. We talk about books, sports, and going on long bike rides. In addition to this, he assists me with the subjects. He acts as a mentor to young men in many different ways. Simply being in his presence inspires me to perform to the best of my abilities.

One thing that immediately struck me about Mr. Simon Weale our new Director at BCS was his approachability. He's not just some distant figure locked away in an office. Instead, he walks around the campus, interacts with students, and listens to our thoughts and ideas. It's as if he genuinely values our opinions and wants us to feel heard.

Mr. Weale is a firm believer, and an ardent supporter in the power of sports and physical activities. He renovated the sports facilities, and we now have a state-of-the-art gymnasium and fields for various outdoor games. His emphasis on overall well-being has encouraged more students to participate in sports, leading to a healthier and happier school community.

1

The day I left my home

Now when I think about the day I left my home, it still gives me colly wobbles. It seemed impossible to start from scratch in a new place, with new people, and with everything new.

March 4, 2017, was the day I was to report to Bishop Cotton School, Shimla.

The journey was long, and my father decided to make it even longer. We drove for four hours from Umroi, a place 17 kilometers away from Shillong to Guwahati, flew from Guwahati to Delhi, before beginning our real journey on a toy train from Kalka to Shimla. I had travelled earlier in a toy train from Siliguri to Darjeeling. It was an amazing experience. Kalka to Shimla took us approximately eight hours, and that was when I was sat down by my parents and was told the major part of it, going away from home.

My parents have been preparing me emotionally and otherwise as well for months to face this. I, on the other hand, was worried about how am I going to do it without my parents around. I have never been away from my mother for a single night.

The only thing that delighted me was to have so many pairs of new shoes, new pairs of in-liners, and half of the day was devoted to sports.

Believe me, all those trunks full of goodies seemed good for just one night.

The day my parents dropped me off somehow went by, but the night was terrible. My parents had taught and trained me for almost everything, but they never taught me how to live a night without them.

I was used to waking up to their kisses and hugs. And that was the toughest part of moving out.

My father gets me a glass of water to wake me up and then comes my mother with a mug full of milk.

That's how my mornings started when I was full-time at home.

To date, I am offered a lukewarm glass of water before I open my eyes, but ahhh! how I miss not getting a mug full of milk in bed (drawbacks of growing up).

Back then (I miss it every single day, but then you get used to and obviously time is a greater eraser), I missed waking up to the bells, not to my mother's peck on my cheeks and forehead.

I must admit here, being a single child brings you so many perks and privileges, disadvantages of being a single child I will discuss later.

Though I was acquainted with everyone in the dorm, I took a long time to make friends with them.

Since the day I reached BCS, March 4, 2017, I started counting on the day, to meet my parents. For straight 45 days, we were not allowed to meet and speak. It was only through letters that we communicated. Those were the toughest days, that I remember. I saw the first snow season, fell ill, and survived without my mother's head massage, and that's when I realized the importance of it and how relaxing it was. Though I still fret about the oiling part despite that, massage any time of the day.

Boarding teaches you survival and almost everything that you need to know in life. It is pretty apparent that boarding schools provide an excellent educational experience. It is more than just a place to sleep, play and study. Boarding schools foster a 24-hour intentional community focused on the growth and development of the students. And you dare not miss any of the bells in 24 hours.

Bishop Cotton School has been an incredible learning experience for the past six years. Living with 500 boys from all over the world forced me to stretch my boundaries, embrace new traditions, and appreciate new perspectives. In between classes, homework, and extracurriculars, we always found time to have some fun and talk about our lives and families. In fact, we all grew into each other's extended families away from home. We became a support system when someone was down and rejoiced with them when they achieved their goals!

If you ask me, I am always homesick; on any given day, I want to return home and live with my parents (This was only till class 6th). But then there were some difficulties, but as I look back on those six years, I remember how they helped me grow and shaped me into the person I am today.

2

I'm Bored Syndrome

Disclaimer: *- To all those who are reading this, I am 14 years old, entered adolescence and I am fully aware of the consequences. The opinions expressed in this article are purely those of the author. They do not purport to reflect the opinions /views and influence*

of my friends and social group. This is an individual experience, reflecting real-life incidents.

Yes, I am plagued by the "I'm Bored Syndrome", and chronically, I'm beating the "I'm bored syndrome", though sometimes the ability and the time to be bored might be beneficial for two reasons.First, it helps the body and conscious mind to repose, allowing the subconscious creative side to take over–some marvelous things can happen when we get bored!

Second, it takes us away from the need to be amused and allows us to become more self-reliant.

I often wonder what, exactly, it is, the boredom syndrome.

Boredom syndrome is a psychological disorder, a common complaint among children and adolescents that produces physical sickness, something that every parent, teacher and sane adult wants to dodge. It is mostly caused by mental and physical underload at work owing to a lack of enough quantitative or qualitative activity. Boredom may be caused by a lack of sleep or nourishment, lack of mental stimulation, and want of choice or control over your daily activities. This is a definition and description by common Indian parents.

My parents tell me that conventional therapy is required to heal this syndrome in my generation.

Now, what is The Conventional Therapy?

A therapy which works for almost any syndrome in the common Indian child, box on the ear (most of us, I mean boys studying in all boys boarding schools, can give you lessons on how to unblock an ear, after being slapped).

My mother claims she never got bored in her childhood. Perhaps because she was never given that greater flexibility to pick what to do with her time. My father's explanations for boredom are even more plentiful and says boredom is ubiquitous. They have only one solution for any kind of boredom, reading or practice. My mother loads me with books to read and my father is a pro in checking my problem-solving skills, he loads me with numericals to solve or asks me to simply go for a run (for him running can solve almost any problem on earth). I wonder how blue they were in their childhood.

But I am glad and grateful, I'm not running from pillar to post for extracurricular activities. The one thing that has happened in the epidemic, you can attend multiple classes sitting at home. Right from coding to public speaking. No space to be bored.

The epidemic has only exacerbated the issue. It is normal practice these days to 'structure' your child's leisure time. As a result, your child's days are frequently jam-packed with extra-curricular activities. And dear parents, if you believe this is a good thing, reconsider!

Yes, I know it is vital for children to have systematized and scheduled activities, but it is also important for them to have some free time to be bored and figure out ways and means to occupy themselves, subsequently, this stimulates their imagination and creativity. This is why several studies have emphasized on the relevance of boredom to the life of a child.

I took a non-violent option. I now don't get bored but want to do something different and "Masti". It is very difficult to define masti (fun and frolic), but I still want to do some masti with my parents.

I'm curious why most parents feel pressured to keep their children engaged constantly.

Our parents were not born in the 21st century, with 101 options to do every minute, instead, they were told exactly what to do every minute of the day.

While few parents do not believe in the concept of over-scheduling, they are frequently perplexed whether or not they are parenting effectively. They also keep you reminded (with consistent shreds of evidence) of the pressure your peer group is handling, while you are not.

So, dear parents, take a deep breath and assist us in identifying what actually fascinates us, as well as creating a nurturing environment in which we may constructively get bored.

3

Favoritism in schools - the teacher-student connection

While the rest of the world is absorbed in reinventing, restructuring, re-engineering, repositioning, reorganizing, and re-everything else, I am immersed in rewriting my thoughts and experiences on favoritism.

Favoritism is inevitable and ubiquitous.

When I think about favoritism, one issue that comes to me is the preference granted to preferred ones (who are not necessarily sweet, intelligent, and well-behaved, but clever) at school.

There is a very fine line between preference (favoritism) and discrimination.

Although preference may pucker your brow in many situations, it is not unlawful. The primary difference between discrimination and favoritism is that discrimination is always illegal.

Discrimination is the process through which two stimuli that vary in some ways are managed differently, whereas favoritism is the act of displaying a preference for something.

Discrimination can range from how they are penalized if they get into trouble compared to others, to how they are given particular support in the classroom with their grades, assignments, activities, and projects. They, like everyone else, put their pants on one leg at a time. So why special treatment!!

While I was fortunate to be spared the misery of parental favoritism, I would want to draw attention to the student-teacher connection and the rich favoritism that occurs there.

I, too, have a list of favorite teachers (who are my role models, and my mother never fails to accuse me of blindly following them and ignoring her opinions), and yes, I have prejudices about how they teach and interact with other students.

I eagerly await their lessons and talks. I don't want to lose out on any opportunities to engage and learn. I often go out of my way to learn more about those topics. I try to be the first person to submit an assignment and always raise my hand to respond. It goes without saying that I am their blue-eyed lad in the classroom (at least it is so in my head) when I say I have favorite teachers. But then I am mostly denied the privileges that I may possibly gain outside of the classroom.

Giving preferential treatment to a person or group, typically at the expense of others, is referred to as favoritism.

Favoritism by a teacher in a classroom might be overt or subtle. Some of the subtler manifestations include a shift in tone and demeanour when speaking, as well as a reduction in attention paid to doubts made by some disfavoured pupils in a classroom. Favorite pupils are given more opportunities than deserving students.

I do not intend to advocate for or against favoritism. Even Dronacharya and Parshurama, the greatest sage and gurus of greatness, exhibited partiality and were accused of favoritism.

There are many instances where Dronacharya has shown favoritism, to Arjuna and Ashwathama. Drona wanted Arjun to be the finest archer and didn't appreciate Eklavya displaying the talent. As his Guru-Dakshina, Dronacharya asked Eklavya to give his right thumb. Eklavya gave it up, knowing he'd never be able to wield his bow and arrow again. Drona also denied mentoring Karna.

So how does favouritism affect here?

Favoritism is usually disguised under a cloak of justifications.

I have experienced that the favoured students mostly resort to bullying others.

Many times, because of favouritism, opportunities are denied to deserving students. These students will start losing self-confidence and motivation.

However, I am too young to scribe my views on such a touchy topic and raise grievances about favouritism, but I do know my fundamental rights and also practice the freedom of speech. How wonderfully my favourite civics teacher taught me in 9th grade.

We students must realise that the teachers are human beings with preferences, likes, and dislikes, just like parents. They are also fallible to some extent. However, if the favouritism becomes too blatant to the point that it interferes with normal class dynamics, the less favoured ones should simply ignore, or cry over for a while and move on with their gang (not so preferred and favoured ones).

What other option do we have?

Yes, getting preferential treatment, for whatever reason, can be infuriating at times.

The other so-called 'average' students also deserve a chance to participate, express or showcase their hidden talents and should be judged without any bias.

The less-than-stellar pupils can be coached and guided to improve their results. This may need patience and time, but the rate of progress will be a rewarding journey as you see a pupil excel.

I always wonder how the favoured student feels.

Do the favoured student(s) ever feel awkward when such favouritism for them becomes too obvious and deliberate?

Or do they fear being teased or even bullied by their peers?

Do they develop colly wobbles because they are afraid of being labelled as "teacher's pet"?

Perhaps, they are too absorbed with the upsides of favouritism. Eager and engaged, enjoying the spotlight.

Meanwhile, I notice myself going green, not from discomfort, but a touch of envy. Am I doubting myself or my attributes, nay there's no probability.

It is only that when I am denied something I deserve or maybe I could achieve with a little help (for some students require a little push or some kind of hook to maximise on their skill and capitalize on their strengths); I feel bad for myself and sometimes ridiculously sad for my parents, who have been sacrificing their comfort for me, their only child.

So, think about it. Our experiences are going to make us look at lessons with an entirely different approach.

P.S. - Leave No Child Behind, help them further rather than favour only a few.

4

Is success an extreme tolerance for failure?

Yes, it is because failure at some point of time in life is inevitable, it is bound to happen no matter how hard we try to avoid it. It allows us to evaluate what we did right and wrong so, we will be better prepared for the next lesson that life throws our way. Failure motivates us and challenges us to do more than we ever imagined. It helps us to brush up on our skills, and forces us, so we can prove ourselves worthy. The knowledge we attain from failure lasts longer than the one we attain from success.

No, I am not on a spiritual, motivational journey. Neither I am here to lecture on this topic nor have I faced enough failures to have mastered this topic.

God forbids!

This is a hot topic for debates and essays. Mrs. Zaidi, my present geography teacher who then taught us English and Geography, assigned this topic to me and my opponent for the debate competition.

It was during the Covid times; I was at home and everything was running online.

This topic intrigued me and I chose to write and speak in favor, as I was aware my opponent would choose to speak against the topic for the simple reason, he has never failed in class or in any competitions. I, on the other hand, never get things in the first go, reasons I know and understand.

Nobody likes to fail. But for a teenager, failure can feel like devastation.

And I missed the debate by a whisker. My opponent was louder than me, and he had better gestures, alas no points for originality. You also score some brownie points because of favoritism. The pros and cons are already mentioned in the book.

What I learned from this failure was I have a flair for writing. And in exchange, I read about many leaders and their stories. The book "How to lead" has stories of renowned leaders. I did not read the book cover to cover but could gather a lot of information.

There have been many occasions when I have been rejected, scored poorly, and lost in games. In one instance, I was thrown out of the event just a couple of hours before it was to start. I was devastated.

I cried to my parents over the phone. I was presenting a poem I wrote that has also been published. Whoever reads it has a grin on their face and leaves me with words of appreciation. But then setbacks, mistakes, miscalculations, and failures are all part of growing up, say my parents.

We must always try it instead of letting it go. It's better to try to not regret it in the future. It is better to do something imperfect rather than do nothing perfectly.

Failure always comes with a pinch of humiliation. I have felt that pain several times. The worst was when I was told not to perform at the eleventh hour. It helps us to discover what we can do and how much we can take.

Not that just losing at the debate and elocution, I am not on a self-realization path. I have faced many failures, right from scoring poorly in certain subjects (the subject, that everyone liked "HINDI"), losing at matches, and facing rejections at school events. This I learned from the several years of being in a boarding school and having faced a lot of things that boys of my age and in a day school would not even know or understand.

"Failure is success in progress," Albert Einstein once said while conducting an experiment. Experiments, by definition, are prone to failure.

Abraham Lincoln failed several times in his life, but he persevered and was elected President twice.

Even Amazon did not become a household name overnight. "I've made billions of dollars of failure," Amazon founder Jeff Bezos said at a conference. Most plans and people fail, as do start-ups and businesses, but failure provides a better perspective. Failure is the key to success.

While researching the subject, I discovered a new term for "fear of failure": Atychiphobia.

Clearly, few teenagers are familiar with that term, but many of them encounter it on a daily basis.

I read somewhere that adolescence is the time when your ego and identity are still forming, and believe me when I say that even the slightest rejection feels like the end of the world. You develop a sense of self-doubt, but your friends who have failed far more than you are there to cheer you up. And, of course, your parents, who will always have your back. There are two things my parents say to me.

My mother would just say that she is glad I tried; console me and ask me to prepare well, always showing me the brighter side.

My father, of course, takes the difficult path says, stick to the fight, and shows me where and why I erred. Why did the other person win? I now realise that they are preparing me for the next and bigger battle. I believe that's their way of encouraging their wounded child to move forward in a healing way.

Ever since we were little kids, we have been taught to avoid failure. We don't see failure as a natural part of life and growing up instead; failure is considered to be a taboo and bane of life. Failure is life's greatest teacher.

In the course of growth, failure is the stepping stone to success. This does not mean that we should expect to fail, but when it comes, just accept it. There are many talented people who face failure time and again because they rely on their talent too much, and they forget the basic rule of persistence and perseverance. Failure also makes us humble and lets us go of our ego.

Failure compels us to invent and innovate, create new ideas, make strategies, and find solutions that probably never existed. Most successful personalities have faced failure in their lives, but we just talk and discuss their journey of success to encourage the next generation. We never talk about their failures. Because we are afraid of the darkest fear, the fear of failure.

Perhaps, it's time we teach the younger generation to embrace failures and learn how to deal with them, because "a lesson learned the hard way is a lesson learned for a lifetime."

I tell my mother after every event I took part in and every competition I failed that I tried.

Success is Failure turned Inside out.

5

Are grades important for a successful life?

Preboard is over, and while I'm wondering what my performance will earn me, I'm also thinking about the consequences of not meeting my parents' and teachers' expectations.

Ah, the dreaded grading system. What would we do without them? They are the be-all and end-all of our educational system. We would be completely at sea without them and unable to gauge our own academic progress. But let's be honest, nobody cares about that as much as their grades. Grades are often seen as the way to get to the land of plenty and the golden ticket to fame and fortune.

Holy hearts, teachers, and parents know this all too well. Parents are aware that their children's future happiness and prosperity depend on their academic success. So, they drill into their children's heads that grades are the most important thing in the world. Forget about being kind, compassionate, or having a good work ethic. All that matters is that you get an A+.

But why are grades so important in the pursuit of a successful life? That is simple. Good grades are a requirement for admission to a reputable college. Without a degree from a good college, it's unlikely that one will land a good job. And without a good job, one won't be able to afford the latest iPhone or fancy car. And let's face it, what's the point of living if you can't flaunt your possessions to others?

Don't fret, though. If you're not naturally gifted in academics, there's always a way to get things done. You just need to find that way (says my mother) and I am in pursuit of the same.

There is another way to achieve good grades apart from hard work, perseverance, and great learning. In fact, forego learning entirely. All you need to know are the answers to the test. Who cares about understanding the material, critical thinking, or problem-solving skills? Just regurgitate what you memorized, and you'll be just fine.

While you are struggling to score good grades, you also need to learn important values like honesty, hard work, and perseverance along with that A+ to be happy and successful.

6

The 5 min syndrome

A prime syndrome affecting enormous population.

Disclaimer: *Commonly and technically known as Procrastination. The most prominent symptoms are Lazy, Uncommitted, and Disorganized. People worldwide from the age group of 5 to 70 are plagued with this syndrome. The effect and level vary. I am mildly plagued by the symptoms but have frequent flare-ups which last until I receive some verbal thrashings. Sometimes a violent pat here and there works wonders (mostly for boys of my age group). These treatments are the author's real-time experiences and are recommended at your own risk.*

The most contagious disease in the entire history of mankind. People who get infected with this syndrome can be very challenging to get cured. The only syndrome in which symptoms give you a momentary pleasure and leave you lazier.

So, I was back home for my much-awaited Diwali break, and lazing around is obvious (coming home after a really long time, only a hosteller would know and understand the happiness).

We were all having a casual dinner-time conversation and my mother asked if I have written something new in the past several months. My father acts as a life saver and diverts the topic, but she still finds a way back to discussion and asks me to write something about the UK visit; succumbing to her demands I agreed.

My mother is after my blood to overcome this syndrome. From dawn to dusk, a conversation between me and my mother.

Mother : Amogh (my pet name) get up. You are getting late

Me : Okay, give me 5 minutes.

Mom: Amogh finish your breakfast. Your class starts in 10 minutes.

Me: Finishing in 5 minutes.

Mom: Amogh, switch off the TV.

Me: Okay, I'll turn it off in 5 minutes.

Mother: Amogh go write an essay.

Me: Yes, mom in 5 minutes.

Mother: Go off to sleep

Me: Okay, give me 5 minutes.

A famous aphorism that my mother constantly reminds me of is "bad habits die hard."

Every time my mother asks me to do something, I always politely accept to perform the task after 5 minutes. No ill intentions there, just the force of habit.

For those who haven't met or interacted with my mother, she is what her name says, very soft-spoken, generous, humble and a true Scorpio by nature (beware)!!

She will generously give me multiples of 5 minutes and also a disclaimer (extravagant, bitterly sweet words) that now this work will not be finished before the fifth day from the moment the task was assigned. Yes, she is a hard-taskmaster but a very gentle human being.

And, yes, she is completely right. As I am resuming to finish this article after 5 days, this has happened to me hundreds of times.

Yes, that's what procrastination is.

But, just as every coin has two sides, the 5-minute syndrome has a brighter side as well. I seemed to have no inkling how to loop the words when I sat down to write about the syndrome, I suffer from in order to better myself.

I wrote, rewrote, and then tried my hit-the-target skills. All in the trash can.

The 5 minutes syndrome, I realized, is our bodies' way of telling us to pause for a moment. To ease into it. To think about other options. I might well overthink myself to the point of paralysis if I have too much time.

Furthermore, delaying can work in your favour. Doing things in haste can result in poor outcomes. Allowing yourself time to consider many options, consulting your gut or trusted advisors (your mind and friends), and truly becoming comfortable with a decision is beneficial. When I find myself delaying a task, it's usually because I'm not completely clear on the purpose or outcome I want. Leaving some breathing room in the decision-making process helps to bring clarity and confidence to the decision.

What one may not realise is that even when you aren't actively working on the task, your mind is collecting ideas and processing information to prepare you for it. That means that when you sit down to do it, you'll have a lot more ideas in your head about how to do it.

I have been pondering over what to write about this syndrome for the past 5 days. Had I written it right away it would have been entirely different, I would not have brought up and faced the other side.

My father sets precedents for punctuality. He never ceases to remind me that punctuality is the politeness of kings. He absolutely abhors the 5 minutes Syndrome. I sometimes admiringly adore this skill and find it challenging to persuade him to try it out. But I am out of luck there. He is a genuine fauji. But I am pretty sure, he would have thoroughly experienced and enjoyed the bliss when he was my age.

And today, as much as I despise admitting it, he always wins this battle. Over the years, he has persuaded me and demonstrated the wonders of -(minus) 5 minutes' syndrome. How the -5 minutes' can benefit you more. The best thing is the Pomodoro technique. This entails alternating between periods of study and rest. For example, you can study for 25-minute stretches with 5-minute breaks in between, and then take a longer 30-minute break after every four study sets.

I can see him smiling from ear to ear.

I am not sure how long I will be in this ecstasy, but one thing is for sure I am for a moment my parents favourite. They don't have an option though! Benefits of being the only child.

So, go ahead, try it out. Listening to your parents and admitting it. Trying not to procrastinate would be worth it.

Let us rejoice in the small lessons that our habit teaches us.

Let us investigate WHY we postpone actions and decisions.

Let's give ourselves some leeway when it comes to getting everything done all of the time.

Let us make progress, move forward, and celebrate accomplishments.

7

Being Only is never lonely

Being an only child has a few incredibly undeniable perks.Primarily, you're bestowed with undivided love and attention, also you're always the favorite child (truly a feeling unmatched).

Because it is just the three of you, you always have a close bond with your parents.

And, I enjoy these perks the most.

Do I need to say more!!

There is also a downside to being an only child.

You have all the attention.

Yes, all the attention round the clock, which means you move an inch, they will notice you. You cannot just do / get away with things. They know how to trap you into the emotional web and get things done their way.

However, society has a neatly packaged preconceived notion of what it is like to be an only child.

Spoiled, selfish, and stubborn are just a few adjectives usually associated with "the only." The idea that only children are automatically bizarre or bratty just because we don't have siblings is so unfair.

As an only child, I'm aware of the reputation that precedes me. And I despise being pitied by the older generation for not having company. On that very occasion, how I wish I could tell them of all the company I have been blessed with.

Here I would like to draw the attention of all those who have been tutoring me and my parents on almost every occasion they get.

I also wonder how parenting problems are cured by having two children instead of one.

And how does that guarantee that having a sibling will make you a better person, and better suited?

The most obvious disadvantage of being an only child is the feeling of loneliness. It can be difficult to not have a sibling with whom they can regularly play or share their thoughts and memories.

I'm not a social butterfly, but I consider myself fortunate to have had and continue to have as many friends. And, as I have previously stated, I'm not at ease spending and investing my emotions, opinions, and thoughts with a larger group of people.

But, I am fortunate to grow up in a big joint family full of people around me, so there was always someone to ride bikes, play board games or play in the park with. I have cousins and the same number of friends as everyone else. All I need is to look outside to find them. My cousins are both older and younger than me. They guide me, and we make fun of each other and throw tantrums. We bicker over, we fight, and we tattletale. We hug, we make up (terms and conditions applied), and we always look out for each other (unconditionally). Even though I am referring to them as cousins here, I have always had them as my siblings.

In fact, I believe that being an only child aided me in focusing even more on friendship. Because I don't have siblings, I've worked hard to cultivate and keep close friends as family.

Coming to the comparison and pressure, while the siblings have to brutally face the comparison, the only child is always under a whole lot of pressure, be it family, teachers, or society. We push ourselves pretty hard, to meet up the expectations.

I have read somewhere that only children are

overpraised which conveniently leads to their heads. Ask me about overpraise.

There's no such word in my parents' vocabulary as overpraised. They know exactly how many words to spend in my praise and appreciation, how much to invest when I have been wrong or underperformed, or just being lazy and not doing what I should.

While I was growing up, I was a lot heavier than I am now. My father, on one fine morning, asked me to try pushups and front rolls. I lazily did and tried to get off with it. The worst thing you can ever say to my father is "I cannot do it," and I regret saying that. He pushed me every morning and the next week I was rolling front and back.

While my father will be rash and rough on me, when such incidents happen, my mother would serve me with her hot and cold treatment. She will gently wipe my tears and sweat off and push me to put in a little extra effort.

I wonder where she gets these attributes from or if it is just their (my parents) planned trick to push me to do things they want me to do.

Whatever it is, I'm always, cherished and coddled. I enjoy having my own space, and I enjoy the closeness that I have with my parents.

Kids who grow up alone aren't loners or introverts, and they don't mind spending time alone.

As an only child, your experience may differ depending on your family's circumstances and your personality. With no siblings around, you have the freedom to choose how you spend your time. You can play alone and develop your imagination and creativity. You might receive more one-on-one attention from your parents. They may have more time to listen to your thoughts, feelings, and ideas.

PS: The constant and undivided attention my parents have given me to date and still continue to, has never left me feeling lonely, even though I am theirs 'Only'.

8

All Hope Is Not Lost

Have you ever considered the pleasure of going 15 days without studying? If you ask me, it's an out-of-this-world sensation. And as we return, I realize what a rut I will be in and how much I will miss these fifteen days.

I'm writing from London while on a cricket tour, sitting in my room, where I was the opening batsman.

We won the match, and I was a duck, wondering what really matters. That we have or that which we do not have and we are in pursuit of.

I am also pondering over the things teachers and parents keep reminding us, or if I may use the word grilling in right from childhood, that "Life is not a bed of roses". You will have challenges along the way.

We live in a world where people face a variety of problems, circumstances, and challenges. Some people survive the challenges, while others do not.

The only difference is that the challenges are different, and the only similarity is the multifarious name "CHALLENGE."

Is life really difficult, or we make it sound and look at it that way?

I guess this is a question that only a few people can answer because a large percentage of people do not have answers. I am having a gamut of thoughts running through my mind if I look at and reflect on the question mindfully.

The question is so weighty (obviously for my age). Every man and woman born into this world is destined for battle because life is full of them (my mother told me once, while she was facing some challenges).

The current challenge I am facing is clicking pictures. There's a bigger challenge too, sharing the pictures with my parents, for I need to filter those. My parents would savor the moments I am experiencing through these pictures. The pictures will be zoomed to the max, to check my expressions, whether I am happy, enthusiastic or lazy, and disappointed. My posture will be checked and corrected as they get the chance.

If they find my hands in the pocket or folded, I am certain to receive a 200 words quick note on the importance of being active/proactive and how your body language defines your state of mind. My daddy takes the lead (obvious reason, the army running in his veins and arteries everywhere) and my mother will start by quoting some famous old age adage or Allan and Barbara, she will never miss a chance to feed my mind with thoughts only she invents and later feeds my mouth with *ladoos* and the nutritious values, which will help me to have better concentration, improved stamina and resulting to be active and healthy. (I wonder how she suddenly gets into that superwoman avatar, is it actually the *ladoos* she makes that works?).

Coming back to the challenges, pictures are never enough. I am grateful to the teachers who were abundantly generous to share ample pictures in the group timely to feed parents' curiosity and to some extent keep them unruffled.

I realised that there is a distinct challenge that parents face, and I frequently wonder how to overcome this challenge. They are never happy or content.

The "Little More Syndrome". Smile a little more, eat a little more, run a little more, and Ah! study a little more. Anything you do, does not matter; you put your best foot forward, and they will always ask for a little more.

What I am now going to confess is the most important part, I realised how important that little more is. How that extra mile helps you reach where your parents have been wishing for all this while.

Wishing requires as much energy as planning.

We can learn just as much from what hasn't worked as we can from what has.

What our parents and teachers tell us is not to scare us, but to prepare us to face the challenges and responsibilities of life, to keep us motivated and focused (which sometimes I find difficult, I conveniently get swayed away by whims and fancies).

The lesson I learned is to strive for excellence rather than perfection. All this time, I've been chasing perfection, which has led nowhere.

"There are two educations. One should teach us how to make a living and the other how to live."

London taught me how to live.

How to live with the bare minimum. Inventory everything and try to have multipurpose items.

It isn't about denying yourself pleasure, it's about finding pleasure in simplicity.

Though here I would confess how tempted I was to buy those white and black Jordan shoes, I was getting at a steal deal. I tried convincing my mother, but she is a tough cookie. I wrote a persuading note that explains to my parents why I deserved what I was trying to get. A few days later, I realized, when I saw boys running out of both money and space, she was right. And I know she will have a big grin on her face whenever she reads this.

I also realized I have a huge obsession with the colors; white and black. Whatever I purchased was either white or black; there was no third option. Grey is, indeed, overrated.

On many occasions, my mother has reminded me of my obsession and urged me to show some interest in other colors. As my mother urges me to understand the colors, I urge her to consider the physics behind these colors, which will be way more pleasing to the mind than to the eyes. It also speaks about my traits, additionally, these are the best colors because white disperses into VIBGYOR, and black absorbs all of them.

I'm not sure how much I'll be translating my thoughts as I land on Mother Earth, but I'll definitely return much more educated, learned, and with life experience.

I also return with debt on my account. I need to return 50 GBP to an Old Cottonian with interest. I was astounded by this gesture of lending all the boys 50 pounds; for me, those 50 pounds were priceless. It also taught me to save pennies for rainy days. I saved that 50 £ for the last day and used them to buy souvenirs for my parents at the airport's duty-free shop.

The sense of accomplishment I felt was immeasurable.

The joy on my parent's faces was profound and unrivaled.

9

Do rats also take part in a rat race?

Rats are famous for nibbling- a natural and necessary survival mechanism.

It can both chew and gnaw, - being able to chew through things—soft concrete, wood, plastic, aluminium, and cinder blocks are no match for these rodents. Their love of chewing is due, in part, to the fact that their teeth never stop growing. In order to keep them from becoming too long, making eating impossible, rats must constantly gnaw to wear down their teeth.

An idiom that seems to have originated in the 1930s in the United States. Rat racing isn't a sporting event. Rats do have a reputation for relentlessness, competitiveness, and speed. This expression's origin is a nautical phrase for a fierce tidal current; rat and race are forms of the French ras, which means "tide-race." "Rat race" suggests a confusing, crowded, useless scramble for survival, and, unfortunately, many people use the phrase to describe their jobs and lives. It is a never-ending, self-defeating, or meaningless pursuit.

The term is generally affiliated with a strenuous, monotonous lifestyle that leaves little time for relaxation or enjoyment.

The phrase compares humans to rats attempting in vain to earn a reward such as cheese. It could also refer to a struggle to get ahead financially or routinely.

The mentioned race is not prevalent in the working group of our parents and elders. Come meet the students (any class/grade). Are they not living a fierce, competitive way of life that involves pursuing goals in a repetitive, endless manner?

We are pushed into this race predominantly and mercilessly.

For all those who agree to disagree. I have a mountain of evidence, done my homework right and well on time. I study in an all-boys boarding school. We are buddies and we discuss our parents and their great varied traits.

Yes, we do that. Talk about all the pressure we go through. If you are not scoring well, then you are pressurised to put in the extra effort. If you are not good academically, you better be a sportsman. If not that, then be an orator or an artist. Basically, achieving the magic algorithm of scores and activities.

Aren't we behaving like rats, in a maze? Doing tricks. Performing chores thought up by somebody else. Somebody is not any random person, it clearly implies to our parents, family, and all the well-wishers. And not to miss your buddies' parents. They would never cease to give you that life lesson and leave no stone unturned to motivate you to flourish. But then there is a catch even when they are motivating you to do well, deep down they are wishing their child to be better than you. We boys very well know that and understand.

I have never met any parents who are sorted and relaxed, with the "we will face the storm" attitude. Who are just perfectly fine with their child not scoring well, or not participating in any of the extracurricular activities!

For boarders like me, who live and grow in a very protected environment, with the same set of minds for over years' day in and out. Everybody knows everybody.

The boys right after the midterm start preparing for the Balieys competition and open prizes, which is all about getting the best grades, being the best at a sport, and partaking in the school's popularity contest. Participating in the sequence of events for two straight months, thinking and working towards it round the clock.

But as we are encouraged to pursue this, we've been pushed into unhealthy and unhappy patterns that are harming a whole generation. I realized it this year when I was part of many events. Every year I find myself better than the previous year, but sadly not good enough.

There are other boys as well, well deserving, who participated in several competitions but could hardly receive a reward to certify their hard work. I wonder where did they lose and I am also left pondering did they lose the power of play in this race and am praying in the race they did not lose hope.

Hoping to get stronger for the next season, I wonder when did we get into this - the incessant pursuit of more. It's difficult to pin down the moment when we joined the rat race. It just sort of...happened.

You are never enough, waiting to reap the fruits of your labor.

I wonder what kind of childhood Mr. Pichai and Nadella would have had. Do they still get into the rat race after achieving almost everything one would ever wish for?

And how about the PM Rishi Sunak. Yes, you have

already earned all the trust and respect you mentioned in your speech.

Here the question is Quit the race or Kill the rat. Is it ok to escape the rat race and still be competitive?

Note that rat race is hyphenated when used as an adjective before a noun.

10

Choices are Many, but Choose Wisely

As I embarked on this new chapter of my life, I couldn't help but feel a mix of excitement and uncertainty. The familiar halls of my beloved boarding school would now be replaced by a different campus, a different environment.

Spending a significant amount of time together with 70 other boys under the same roof, and living in a boarding school setting can foster close relationships with fellow students and faculty members. These relationships often extend beyond the academic setting and can form life-long friendships. Boarding schools also typically offer a wide range of extracurricular activities and opportunities for personal growth, which can contribute to a well-rounded education. And I was apprehensive about the changes.

Choosing the school closer to home allowed me to pursue my passion while also staying connected with my roots. I realized that my desire to explore the world could still be fulfilled in different ways. I could travel during breaks, immerse myself in different cultures through books and documentaries, and even participate in exchange programs or internships later on.

I soon discovered that the school I chose had its own unique charm. The teachers were inspiring and knowledgeable, and I found a community of like-minded individuals who shared my interests. The proximity to my family provided me with a strong support system, which proved to be invaluable during challenging times.

While some of my friends ventured far away to pursue their dreams, I found solace in knowing that I had made a decision based on what truly mattered to me. I understood that success wasn't solely determined by the distance traveled, but rather by the dedication and passion I brought to my chosen path.

Every day, as I attended classes and engaged in discussions with my peers, I realized that my decision had opened up new opportunities. The school's location allowed me to connect and explore prospects that aligned with my interests.

As time passed, I grew more confident in my decision. I saw the impact of my choices and the opportunities that unfolded before me. I learned that life is a series of decisions, each leading us down a different path. While some choices may seem daunting, it is in these moments that we must trust ourselves and follow our instincts.

Looking back now, I am grateful for the advice I received from Mr. Bhatt and the courage to choose wisely. It was a reminder that life is a journey, and the choices we make shape our experiences and define our happiness. I understood that choosing a path that aligned with my values and passions would ultimately lead me to a fulfilling and purposeful life.

So, as I sit here reflecting on my journey, I am filled with gratitude for the choices I made. The road may have been different from what I initially imagined, but it has led me to a place of growth, self-discovery, and fulfillment. Choices are indeed abundant, but when we choose wisely, we create a life that resonates with our true selves.

11

The Exquisite Art of Indian Parenting

Disclaimer: This write-up is intended purely for humour and should not be taken as a reflection of all Indian parents or their qualities. Parenting styles and individual experiences vary greatly, transcending cultural boundaries.

India has a diverse population with varying religious, political, and cultural perspectives on child-rearing practices. With so many disparities among Indians, it is impossible to attribute a cohesive set of child-rearing habits and beliefs to the entire country. The influence of financial background, education, and individual experience on upbringing practices varies from family to family.

But one thing remains the same, in the land of endless expectations and stern expressions, exists the quintessential Indian parents, with their unwavering determination to shape their children into perfect beings, they are a force to be reckoned with. It is pretty pertinent to remember that this determination is driven by love, concern, and a desire to see their children succeed.

The board exam results are out and the exchange of calls and texts between parents is at its peak, discussing what and how. In this momentous event that occurs once a year, Indian parents from all corners of the country have been observed going through a whirlwind of emotions.

As the results are announced, Indian parents transform into walking, talking calculators. They meticulously calculate percentage points, class rank, and potential college admission possibilities, armed with pens, papers, and furrowed brows. They can be observed crunching numbers, analysing patterns, and performing statistical analyses worthy of mathematicians.

It is often mentioned and debated in various forums that the outcomes are interconnected within and across diverse domains of development, do they really mean it.

While my parents are a little considerate, but they still have some peculiar qualities, which define and categorise them as typical Indian Parents. My mother chooses her timings and words very wisely. She puts her point ruthlessly and makes it amply clear. But, this is not done in a go. She keeps coming with different sets of motivational and pep talks.

My father is way smarter than her in certain areas, and has honed guilt-tripping to an art form.

With a single sigh, he can make you feel like you've disappointed generations of ancestors. Your failure to comply with their wishes is equivalent to defying the laws of gravity.

No matter how hard you try, you'll always be one choice away from crushing their dreams and plunging the entire universe into chaos.

Not that I have scored poorly in my Boards. Let me put it differently. I have scored way more than what they have. But then again, the great Indian parents, they make the rules and they break it too.

Indian parents are connoisseurs of comparison. They believe that their child's true potential is only revealed when placed beside their coursemate's son or their cousins and relative's daughter or any XYG they have ever known. No achievement is ever sufficient unless it outshines the accomplishments of these fictional benchmarks.

For a moment even if your parents are marginally happy if not exceptionally, the other parents would not miss a chance and barge into the moment to ruin it forever. Beware the dreaded line: "Sharma Ji ka beta/ beti!"

These Indian parents possess qualities so remarkably distinct that they create an indelible mark on their children's lives, forever shaping their destinies.

Then there is the other set of Indian parents - Degree-Driven Dynamos: they are often obsessed with their child's academic achievements.

Indian parents have an intrinsic ability to develop their children's potential. They are the masters of ambition, encouraging their children to thrive in academics, extracurricular activities, and pretty much anything else that will give them bragging rights at the next family gathering. They believe in producing prodigies, even if it means depriving their children of sleep, play-time, and social interactions.

They firmly believe that a high GPA is the key to success in life. No matter the situation, their unwavering focus remains on ensuring their child becomes an engineer, doctor, MBA graduate, or entrepreneur (it is mostly the first two options). After all, who needs dreams and aspirations when you can have a stable job and societal validation?

This kind doesn't just stick to their children, they never miss a chance to tell the other parent how successful they as parents are because their *Aankhon ka Taara* has scored highest.

I believe this set of Indian parents is obsessed with their social status and standing in the community. The opinions and judgments of others hold immense power over their decisions.

They must ensure their child's achievements, appearances, and life choices reflect positively on the family's reputation. The fear of *"log kya kahenge"* (what will people say) governs their every move which is not restricted to just their child. They will not miss a chance to corrupt the other EASY going parents' minds and souls.

These frequent sessions between parents pre and post exams lead to the Sacrifice Sagas.

Indian parents love to remind their children of the countless sacrifices they've made. From relinquishing their own dreams to working tirelessly to provide a better life, they never let their child forget their debt of gratitude. Guilt-tripping is their secret weapon, designed to ensure their child never strays from the path they've carefully paved.

Indian parents seem to possess a remarkable ability to wear multiple hats simultaneously. It's as if they have mastered the art of being a psychologist, counselor, coach, nutritionist, and soothsayer all at once. I wonder how they manage to juggle these roles; wear so many hats all at the same time.

Do parents ever think about the children? How is it for the child?

Growing up amid the frenzy of Indian parenting as an Indian child is like setting off on an uncharted journey full of unexpected twists and turns. It seems like a never-ending dance that involves love and exasperation, tradition and modernity, and expectations and individualism.

Remember, dear readers, while my expressions may highlight some exaggerated traits (but carries a grain of truth), it is essential to recognize the love, care, and good intentions that underlie the actions of our parents. Their aspirations stem from a desire for their children to succeed and find happiness, albeit in their own unique way. Beneath all the occasional frustration and misunderstandings, there is an undeniable love that permeates Indian parenting. It is often expressed through doting gestures, nourishing meals, and unwavering support during challenging times. We may not always see eye-to-eye with our parents, but their love is a constant, providing a sense of security and warmth that shapes our sense of belonging.

12

Chemistry: The unsolved Mystery of life

Disclaimer: *To all those reading, you would be wondering why does a book have something related to chemistry and why do we have to read chemistry here. How is chemistry related to my journey? It is very much related (If you are a science student you will be able to relate it more).*

The subject that has all the branches of science in it (it has more complicated calculations than mathematics), it has biology and physics. From stars to tranquil streams, it weaves the fabric of life's grand schemes. It is nature's cosmic ballroom where it is always under the spotlight. The atoms along with Dalton's Atomic theory gracefully welcome us in class 6. We all think that chemistry is a cake-walk. Don't be in a hurry because you are sadly mistaken. The fundamental of chemistry then matter classification, this might all look easy and it's the easiest in 6th, actually in the entire chemistry. But by the time we understand Dalton's theory, we realized that now it is class 7. Here the electrons, protons, etc. are waiting to traumatize you along with Rutherford's gold leaf experiment and plum pudding (WHO PUTS CHEMISTRY IN FOOD and this is the first thought in your mind), then comes JJ Thompson and other GREAT SCIENTISTS, but you overcome and adjust yourselves in 7th, to hear that whatever we studied in 6th is wrong. Fast-forwarding to 10 (until 10, half of the chemistry is fake or proved wrong). Now in 10th, we actually study something that is related to chemistry but now with mathematics (it does not include a lot of mathematical applications but a lot of calculations and by a lot I mean numbers going up to 10 to the power of 23). MOLE CONCEPT here comes another nightmare. (it's not that hard though).

We all passed 10th with flying colors in chemistry.

Now the 11th, we study Lewis dot structure, Niels Bohr, Heisenberg's uncertainty, more physics and mathematics, etc. Again to realize that Lewis dot structure was wrong. Then we come to know that atoms don't even have their shells / orbit, the probability of finding the electron is 0% somewhere and somewhere 95%.

By this time, we are all uncertain whether chemistry is real or not.

What comes next, I can narrate only when I get there.

And hats off to those who fall in love with Chemistry and also plan to be married.

My first Chemistry teacher, Mrs Deborah Anothny, is an amazing teacher and she is the one who introduced me to this subject, and I fell in love with the subject at first sight, so much so that I was studying, talking and dreaming Chemistry.

But who knew then that this subject is just like my mother, changes its course of action as per its convenience.

And, imagine the status of a boy whose father is a chemistry geek, you reach him with a difficulty in the subject and he very comfortably narrates the entire process only to leave you even more disillusioned and partially starry-eyed, for you have someone to fall back.

13

Embracing the Change : The journey of changing school

Change, life's elusive chameleon, has a knack for surprising us when we least expect it. So, it was when I was faced with the difficult prospect of switching schools after 6 years.

On this rocky voyage, I was in for a rollercoaster of emotions, and as I went into this new route, I couldn't help but worry if I was prepared to accept the unknown.

A school is a sacred place where the echoes of generations past mingle with the ardent murmurs of the present. Our parents have gone through this rite of passage, and they speak of it with nostalgia and wisdom. They may, however, be unaware of the labyrinth of problems and tribulations that this modern generation experiences with each twist and turn of change.

The world today evolves at an unparalleled rate, and we are assaulted with novelties as we enter the hallways of our educational institutions. Technological innovations have disrupted traditional learning limits, with information at our fingertips. The continual flow of information leaves us gasping for air, unable to separate fact from fiction in an ever-expanding digital universe.

It is difficult to adjust to any change. I know, there aren't many changes in a child's life. However, those changes may be difficult for the children to adjust to. "Changing Schools" is the most prevalent change. This is the most dreaded alteration; it's a student's worst nightmare. We had to leave behind the positive memories we had of that school, the fun events we participated in, and the friends we grew up with. And the teachers who were adored.

Changing schools is a crucial and difficult event in a student's life, as it means saying goodbye to old friends and making new ones. Unaware of their surroundings, people and teachers "IN THE NEW SCHOOL".

Leaving familiar and comfortable surroundings behind is an emotional turmoil. And I can tell you all of this from personal experience (because my father is an Army officer, and every 18 to 24 months, he moves and I have to change schools, which is one of the reasons I went to boarding school).

Making new acquaintances is difficult for some people, but if you have been moving schools, it is simple (I have changed 11 schools, which is a lot).

DPS VK is my 11th, and I'll be here for Upper Sixth, which will mark the conclusion of my school career and prepare me for the next roller-coaster ride.

Meanwhile, I attended Modern School for a short time and wondered how quickly I adjusted to the change, (hoping that now I won't have to change any more schools). There, I was able to interact nicely; boys assisted me in whatever way they could. MSVV has left me with some pleasant recollections.

In the midst of the anxiety, I couldn't help but notice the ridiculousness in some circumstances. I felt like a specimen being examined and dissected under a microscope with fascinated eyes. It felt like I was in a bumbling comedy show every time I fumbled over my words or got lost trying to find my way to a classroom. Maybe the school should have provided me with my own laugh track to accompany my gaffes.

Probably, in the midst of the tumult of change, there will be serendipitous moments that will shape my perspective. Hopefully, I'll meet like-minded people who will become my allies on this perilous voyage. We'd negotiate the perilous waters of adolescent turmoil, hilariously terrible cafeteria cuisine, and convoluted passageways that looked engineered to snare naive kids.

In the midst of it all, I learned that embracing change was about building my own path in the midst of chaos rather than fitting into a preset pattern.

So, dear reader, my school-change journey was one of emotional upheaval, self-discovery, and the conclusion that life, with all of its quirks and oddities, can be a satirical masterpiece. Accepting change meant submitting to chaos and finding laughter in the most unlikely of situations.

When I think back on this journey, I can't help but grin and enjoy the memories that have formed me into the person I am today. So, here's to embracing change and laughing in the thick of it all!

14

Almost Adult

As I take my first step into the glorious realm of 16, I felt it's about time we have a little heart-to-heart. You know, a moment of reflection on how my life has unfolded so far. I feel it's my duty to share my thoughts and observations with you. You see, dear Mom and Dad, I must commend you on raising a responsible and ambitious young lad.

But then, I have to admit, there are times when I wonder if life would be a bit more adventurous if I were like some of my buddies. So, with my tongue firmly planted in my cheek, let me present my plea on how things could be different.

Don't worry; I promise to be gentle with my sarcasm, disciplined and not to violate the family values and ethics.

Let's start with my grand vision of how life would be at 16, and how my 16th birthday would be celebrated. In my visions, I envisioned myself receiving a smartwatch packaged in a stylish gift box, as well as a pair of Air Jordan 38 and a Couture Deluxe Tuberose.

Being the coolest kid in town, surrounded by loving peers (from Modern School, DPS VK, and, of course, BCS Shimla). But, alas, I must thank you for the life lessons you taught me by putting those goals into perspective.

What I envisioned: a smartwatch wrapped in an exquisite present box, a pair of Air Jordan 38, and a Couture Deluxe Tuberose with the wind in my hair, turning heads as I passed by.

What I got: a few drops of your regular Versace perfume, a pair of Beverley Hill shoes, and the same old GShock.

Moving on, let's talk about my social life. In an ideal world, I'd be the life of every party (ask my Modern School buddies) and have people lined up to be my friend. Once again, your grand plan appears to be steering me in the wrong path.

What I envisioned was throwing amazing parties to which everyone would want to be invited.

What I got: A small birthday party at Barbeque Nation with a few obligated pals.

Let us now discuss the allowance you provide. My aspirations of receiving a large sum of money at the age of 16 have been completely dashed.

What I imagined: an endless supply of cash, sufficient to buy anything I want/desire and swimming in cash like Scrooge McDuck.

What I got: A pittance that hardly supports my basic needs and sorry son, we have a budget, and you need to learn to manage your money wisely.

And can we discuss liberty? At 16, I assumed the world would be my oyster, and I'd be able to stretch my wings and conquer the universe. But, as is customary, reality decided to meddle.

What I envisioned: complete freedom to stay out as late as I wanted and travel wherever I pleased.

What I got: a severe curfew, a GPS tracker on my phone that you constantly check, and weekend JEE preparation classes.

Finally, let's talk about my room and academic performance.

I imagined a beautiful, elegant haven that would be the envy of every teen on the block. Thank you for, well, "helping" me attain that goal.

What I envisioned was a room straight out of a magazine.

What I got: A room that looks like a 90's, with half of my belongings being old toys and stuffed animals I haven't touched in years, books where ever you see and Mom's regular dose of "A clean environment reflects a clean mind".

What I imagined: Well done, my son.

What I got: Young man, responsibilities come first, good food and proper rest is must for a brighter future.

Finally, Mom and Dad, I must say that your amazing ability to keep my dreams from becoming too large for their britches has been an eye-opening experience. While it's been a wild ride, I appreciate you keeping my feet on the ground, even if it means I can't soar like an eagle just yet.

Don't worry; despite the caustic tone of my letter, I still adore you both. I know you have my best interests at heart, and I appreciate the refuge and assistance you provide.

Maybe one day I'll grow up to be a responsible, ambitious world-changer who isn't afraid to occasionally pursue thrills and adventure, and I'll make you both proud.

Who knows, maybe one day, my dreams will align with reality—well, a kid can hope, right?

Love,

Your Responsible (and occasionally cheeky) Teen.

P.S. Can I at least have pizza, coke and ice cream for breakfast on my birthday?

15

Dolce Far Niente

In a world when time is a valuable commodity, the Italian adage "dolce far niente" provides a refreshing perspective on life. This lovely term, which translates to "the sweet art of doing nothing," captures the essence of appreciating the moments, finding contentment in stillness, and revelling in the pleasures of life at a slower pace. To properly comprehend the art of dolce far niente, we must go deep into its origins, investigate its profound meanings, and uncover how it might be incorporated into our modern life.

The Italian culture has a long history and is well-known for its contributions to art, cuisine, and lifestyle. Among its numerous assets, dolce far niente attests to the Italians' intrinsic ability to find beauty and joy in simplicity and idleness.

The phrase is a lyrical combination of three words: "dolce" (sweet), "far" (to do), and "niente" (nothing). Dolce far niente, at its core, encapsulates the belief that true contentment rests not in always trying and doing, but in pausing to relish life's transitory pleasures. It's the delicious beauty of doing nothing and letting the universe unfold at its own speed.

When I was first introduced to this adage, I was clearly told that Dolce far niente is not a praise of sluggishness or an invitation to waste time. Instead, it is a celebration of deliberate idleness, in which one's ideas and feelings take precedence over the logical intellect. You are not bored in these moments, but rather intensely engaged with the present, allowing oneself to get taken away by the beauty of reality.

My parents shared the profound wisdom of dolce far niente not with the intention of transforming me, but to rescue me from the incessant glow of the blue screen and the endless hours of sedentary living.

Dolce far niente serves as a sad reminder of the significance of disconnecting from the digital world in a society dominated by the incessant buzz of technology. While social media and television provide amusement and connectivity, they also absorb a significant amount of personal time and energy. To fully live the Italian way, we must learn to disconnect from the digital world and reconnect with the physical world around us.

Rest has long been considered as important by religion and various cultural traditions. Many religions designate a day of rest and meditation each week, whether it is Friday, Saturday, or Sunday. This activity exemplifies the common human desire for refreshment and reflection.

In today's fast-paced society, the desire of productivity frequently overshadows the importance of relaxation. We've been taught that constant activity is the key to success, leaving little room for restorative inactivity. However, dolce far niente challenges this paradigm by recognizing that all work and no play might really make life dull.

Incorporating dolce far niente into our daily lives may appear difficult at first, especially for those who are accustomed to the continuous pursuit of productivity(with productivity I mean solving test papers after test papers). However, it is a practice that may be gradually fostered and assimilated.

My parents always suggest me to begin by allotting modest periods of time each day for mindful idleness(that is to learn to survive without mobile phone). Resist the impulse to check your phone, email, or social media during these times. Instead, locate a quiet place, close your eyes, and simply be. Concentrate on your breathing and the sensations around you, and allow your thoughts to flow freely and without judgment.

By now dear readers, you all would have known my father well, he is a fitness enthusiast who encourages to go out for a run and walk, for nature heals faster and is the ideal setting for experiencing dolce far niente. Take stroll in the park, trek in the mountains, or relax by the water. Allow yourself to be engulfed by the natural world's beauty and let go of the desire to always be doing something.

Set aside specified times to disengage from the digital world. Unplugging from devices, whether for a few hours each evening or for an entire weekend, can help you rediscover the joy of real-life interactions and leisurely moments.

It reminds us that the joy of life is found not only in accomplishment and busyness, but also in the exquisite art of doing nothing purposefully. We may incorporate this philosophy into our lives and experience the true spirit of dolce far niente by embracing times of conscious idleness, withdrawing from the digital world, and relishing the present.

Dolce far niente is ultimately an appeal to slow down, appreciate life's transitory moments, and find contentment in the pleasant doing of nothing. It is a celebration of the beauty that emerges when we allow ourselves to simply be, free of the demands of a fast-paced world.

So, as we traverse the intricacies of modern life, don't forget to take a moment to halt, breathe, and taste the pleasure of dolce far niente.

The Ageing
Black Beast

Master Anutsek Pathak

Dear Mom and Dad,
I guess the following reasons are good enough to buy a new bike for your
Only Son.

As we embark on our morning walk,
Through the overpass and the park,
We discuss and we talk,
 I ask my mother, About the things I like
And I ask my father to get me a new bike,
With gears and disc brakes
He said, "Give me reasons five"
Though on my black beast,
I like to roll all day long,
But it is sometimes sad,
And often gets mad.
It has started to show the signs of aging,
I guess it has got degenerative diseases,
I know some can be cured,
But no, not always,
Some lead to everlasting disabilities
The tyres and the tubes,
Show signs of imbalance,
Getting cramps and weariness
The shockers,
Show signs of Arthritis,
Joints have stiffness,
And a decreased range of motion,
The chain shows signs of Arteriosclerosis,
Restricting the flow of lubricant,
Sudden numbness and weakness,
The redness of the metallic frame,
Shows an invasion of cancerous cells,
The Brake and gears,

Lack efficiency and suppleness,
Show signs of Multiple sclerosis,
Sometimes it gets confused,
Causing communication problems,
Between the paddles,
And the rest of the parts

I give 'em reasons countless,
Reasons, why the ageing black beast
Needs now to rest,
to be swapped with,
the new and the best.